by
Barbara Getty & Inga Dubay

Handwriting Success™
Portland, Oregon USA

GETTY-DUBAY® ITALIC HANDWRITING SERIES

BOOK A ▪ Basic Italic
14 mm body height

BOOK B ▪ Basic Italic
11 mm, 9 mm body height

BOOK C ▪ Basic & Cursive Italic
9 mm, 6 mm body height   Introduction to Cursive Italic

BOOK D ▪ Basic & Cursive Italic
6 mm, 5 mm body height

BOOK E ▪ Basic & Cursive Italic
6 mm, 5 mm, 4 mm body height

BOOK F ▪ Basic & Cursive Italic
6 mm, 5 mm, 4 mm body height

BOOK G ▪ Basic & Cursive Italic
5 mm, 4 mm body height

INSTRUCTION MANUAL

FOURTH EDITION with SUPPLEMENT
© Copyright 2020 by Handwriting Success, LLC
ISBN 978-0-9827762-0-9

THIRD EDITION
Copyright 1994 by Barbara M. Getty and Inga S. Dubay
SECOND EDITION
Copyright 1986 by Barbara M. Getty and Inga S. Dubay
REVISED EDITION
Copyright 1980 by Barbara M. Getty and Inga S. Dubay
FIRST EDITION
Copyright 1979 by Barbara M. Getty and Inga S. Dubay

All rights reserved.
This text may not be reproduced in whole or in part
without the express written permission of the copyright holder.
Getty-Dubay is a registered trademark in the United States.

Third printing with supplement 2024

Handwriting Success, LLC
Portland, Oregon USA

Distributed by Allport Editions
716 NE Lawrence Avenue
Portland, Oregon 97232 USA
www.allport.com

Printed in the United States of America with no-VOC inks using solar power.

Fonts: Getty-Dubay® Fonts by Handwriting Success™, Learning Curve by Blue Vinyl Fonts,
Lucida Sans and Lucida Schoolbook Italic by Monotype.
Cover Design: Sinda Markham
Front cover picture: Aspen trees, Nevada
Back cover pictures: Coyote in winter; bee on tansy flower

CONTENTS

iv	Introduction
v	Getty-Dubay® Italic Alphabet
vi	Reminders
viii	Assessment Pre-test/Post-test

Getty-Dubay® Basic Italic

1	Lowercase Families 1 & 2
2	Lowercase Families 3 & 4
3	Lowercase Families 5 & 6
4	Lowercase Families 7 & 8
5	Lowercase • a, b, c, d
6	Lowercase • e, f, g, h
7	Lowercase • i, j, k, l
8	Lowercase • m, n, o, p
9	Lowercase • q, r, s, t
10	Lowercase • u, v, w, x
11	Lowercase • y, z
12	Capitals • A, B, C, D
13	Capitals • E, F, G, H
14	Capitals • I, J, K, L
15	Capitals • M, N, O, P
16	Capitals • Q, R, S, T
17	Capitals • U, V, W, X
18	Capitals • Y, Z
19	Sentences • endings: -s, -ing, -ed
20	Numerals & words 0–7
21	Numerals & words 8–10
22	Days of the Week
23	Sentences • question & answer
24	Months of the Year • Jan–June
25	Months of the Year • July–Dec
26	Sentences • The Seasons
27	Sentences • big, bigger, biggest
28	Quotations
29	Basic Italic Review—6 mm
30	Numerals & words 0–11
31	Numerals & words 12+
32	Tongue Twisters
33	Tongue Twisters
34	Contractions
35	Homophones
36	Compound Words
37	Compound Words

Getty-Dubay® Cursive Italic

38	Transition to Cursive Italic
39	Transition to Cursive Italic
40	Exit serifs
41	Entrance serifs & exit serifs
42	Cursive Italic—Join 1
43	Cursive Italic—Join 1
44	Cursive Italic—Join 2
45	Cursive Italic—Join 2
46	Cursive Italic—Join 2
47	Cursive Italic—Join 2
48	Cursive Italic—Join 2
49	Cursive Italic—Join 2
50	Cursive Italic—Joins 3 & 4
51	Cursive Italic—Join 5
52	Cursive Italic—Join 5
53	Review Joins 1–5
54	Sentence Practice
55	Cities of the United States
56	Cities of the United States
57	Cities of the United States
58	Sentence Practice
59	A Favorite Letter
60	Supplement—Reading Looped Cursive
62	Letter Lines
63	9mm Blank Lines
64	7mm Blank Lines

INTRODUCTION TO GETTY-DUBAY® ITALIC HANDWRITING

This is the third of seven workbooks in the *Getty-Dubay® Italic Handwriting Series* providing instruction in basic italic handwriting and is the first book in which cursive italic is introduced. Book C is designed for grade two and would also be suitable for the latter part of grade one or early grade three. It may also provide an appropriate program for the learning disabled student or for the person who is learning English as a second language.

This book is not intended as a reading program; written communication is indeed composed of words and sentences – not merely isolated letters. Consequently, it is designed to provide the student with meaningful handwriting experiences. To demonstrate some of the practical ways we use letters, included are: modes of transportation, given names, days of the week, months of the year, seasons of the year, quotations, tongue twisters, contractions, homophones and compound words.

TEACHER/STUDENT INSTRUCTIONS: Writing process/stroke information, directions, notes, reminders, options and assessments are included on student pages. Further letter and join descriptions and assessment questions are found in the INSTRUCTION MANUAL. Each page of this book is designed for the writer to trace the models, then write letters, words and/or sentences in the spaces provided. On some pages the writer completes a given line by writing a "best" letter in the empty box. The pencil is the standard writing tool, but other tools such as the fiber-tip pen may be used. In addition to the review of basic italic, an introduction to cursive italic is presented to assist the student in learning the fundamentals of the cursive hand. The first five of eight joins are presented in BOOK C. The complete Getty-Dubay® basic and cursive italic handwriting program is presented in BOOKS D, E, F and G. See an important note to instructor on page 39.

ASSESSMENT: Assessment is the key to improvement. Our self-assessment method enables the student to monitor progress. This LOOK, PLAN, PRACTICE format provides self-assessment skills applicable to all learning situations. STEP 1: the student is asked to LOOK at the writing and affirm what is the best. Questions are asked requiring a yes/no answer. 'Yes' is affirmation of a task accomplished. 'No' indicates work to be done. Step 1 is used in BOOK C.

CLASSROOM MANAGEMENT: Using direct Instruction, present about two pages a week, with follow-up practice on lined paper. Demonstrate the process/stroke sequence for letters and joins. This instruction, together with opportunities for integrating handwriting into other areas of curriculum, can provide 25 to 40 minutes of practice, 4 to 5 times a week.

From day one, have DESK STRIPS and WALL CHART in place. For extra practice use GETTY-DUBAY® BLACKLINE MASTERS. Have lined paper available that matches the 9mm and 6mm lines used in this book (see Reminders). Lines at the back of the INSTRUCTION MANUAL may be duplicated. Write on the lines provided in this book or use thin paper for tracing over models. It is essential that the instructor provide an understanding of the use of the dot and the arrow to assist the student in completing the pages successfully. It is recommended that the letters and vocabulary be reviewed with the student before turning to the assigned page.

Teach "All letters start at the top and go down or over except lowercase **d** and **e**." Begin each writing session with this sentence, saying it out loud with the students. Emphasize the importance of closing up the tops of **a**, **d**, **g**, **q** and **o** as well as the numerals **0**, **5**, **8** and **9**. This Fourth Edition presents join options and lift options for students to consider. We hope your students enjoy these lessons as they learn or refine their basic italic skills and begin cursive italic!

See INSTRUCTION MANUAL for more information.

·abcdefghijklmnopqrstuvwxyz·

GETTY-DUBAY® ITALIC HANDWRITING SERIES
BASIC & CURSIVE ITALIC ALPHABET

BASIC ITALIC

*All letters written in one stroke unless otherwise indicated. All letters start at the top except lowercase **d** and **e**.*

Aa Bb Cc Dd Ee Ff Gg

Hh Ii Jj Kk Ll Mm

Nn Oo Pp Qq Rr Ss Tt

Uu Vv Ww Xx Yy Zz

0 1 2 3 4 5 6 7 8 9

CURSIVE ITALIC

*All letters written in one stroke unless otherwise indicated. All letters start at the top except lowercase **d** and **e**.*

Aa Bb Cc Dd Ee Ff Gg

ana bnb cnc dnd ene fnf gng
or ene

Hh Ii Jj Kk Ll Mm

hnh ini jnj knk lnl mnm
or knk   or mnm

Nn Oo Pp Qq Rr Ss Tt

nnn ono pnp qnq rnr sns tnt
or nnn   or rnr   or sns

Uu Vv Ww Xx Yy Zz

unu vnv wnw xnx yny znz
or xnx

GETTY-DUBAY® ITALIC HANDWRITING REMINDERS

PENCIL HOLD
Use a soft lead pencil (#1 or #2) with an eraser. Hold the pencil with the thumb and index finger, resting on the middle finger. The upper part of the pencil rests near the large knuckle.

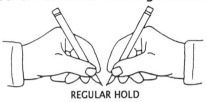
REGULAR HOLD

Hold the pencil firmly and lightly. AVOID pinching. To relax your hand, tap the index finger on the pencil three times.

Problem grips such as the 'thumb wrap' (thumb doesn't touch pencil) and the 'death grip' (very tight pencil hold) make it difficult to use the hand's small muscles. To relieve these problems, try this alternative pencil hold.

ALTERNATIVE HOLD

Place the pencil between the index finger and the middle finger. The pencil rests between the index and middle fingers by the large knuckles. Hold the pencil in the regular way at the tips of the fingers.

PAPER POSITION

LEFT-HANDED

If you are left-handed and write with the wrist below the line of writing, turn the paper clockwise so it is slanted to the right as illustrated. If you are left-handed and write with a "hook" with the wrist above the line of writing, turn the paper counter clockwise so it is slanted to the left as illustrated. (Similar to the right-handed position)

RIGHT-HANDED

If you are right-handed turn the paper counter-clockwise so it is slanted to the left as illustrated.

POSTURE
Rest your feet flat on the floor and keep your back comfortably straight without slumping. Rest your forearms on the desk. Hold the workbook or paper with your non-writing hand so that the writing area is centered in front of you.

LINED PAPER CHOICES
The following choices for lined paper may be used when instructions say use lined paper for practice:

1. Lines with 9mm and 7mm body height (the distance from the baseline to the waistline) are on page 63 and 64. These may be duplicated or they may be used as guides under a sheet of unlined paper. Fasten with paper clips.

    9 mm

2. Lines with a 6mm body height are included in the INSTRUCTION MANUAL. These may be duplicated or used as guidelines under a sheet of unlined paper. Fasten with paper clips.

    6 mm

3. Some school paper has a solid baseline and a dotted waistline. Use paper with a body height of approximately 9mm ($^3/_8$") or 6mm ($^1/_4$").

    6 mm

4. If notebook paper is being used select wide-ruled paper with a space of about 9mm ($^3/_8$") between lines for the first half of BOOK C and college-ruled notebook paper with a space of about 7mm approximately ($^1/_4$") for the second half of BOOK C.

    9 mm

    7 mm

INSTRUCTOR NOTE: These reminders are written for the student, but since most BOOK C writers are early readers, please convey the above information to them in your own words.

VOCABULARY

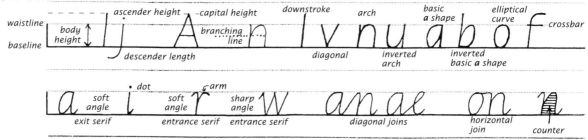

STROKES

Basic italic letters all start at the top and go down or over (horizontal), except **d** and **e**, (**d** starts at the waistline and **e** starts at the center of the body height). If a dot is provided, place pencil on dot then follow the direction of the arrow. Letters are written in one stroke unless otherwise indicated. Trace the solid line model, then the dotted line model, and then copy model in space provided.

LETTER DIMENSIONS

SHAPE:
Basic italic lowercase letters are divided into eight families according to shape. Basic italic capitals are divided into three width groups. Cursive italic lowercase joins are divided into eight join groups. The first five joins are introduced in BOOK C.

SIZE:
Letters are written with a consistent body height. Capitals, ascenders and descenders are written one and a half times the body height.

SLOPE:
The models are written with a 5° letter slope. A consistent slope is an important part of good handwriting. For individual slope choices see *Slope Guidelines* in the INSTRUCTION MANUAL.

SPACING:
Letters are written close together within words. Joins are natural spacers in cursive italic; when lifts occur, keep letters close together. Spacing between words is the width of an **m** in basic italic and the width of an **n** in cursive italic.

SPEED:
Write at a comfortable rate of speed. (Though speed is not a primary concern at this level, advanced students may use the *Timed Writing* in the INSTRUCTION MANUAL as suggested for BOOKS D–G.)

GOAL
To write legible, neat handwriting.

IMPROVEMENT
Assessment is the key to improving handwriting. In this book we introduce the first of the three steps in the **LOOK, PLAN, PRACTICE** self-assessment process.

LOOK: The students look at their own writing and answer any questions on the page.

 The pencil indicates the student is to make a written response to the question, generally by circling "yes" or "no".

 The teacher may encourage students to award themselves a star at the top of the page when they notice self-improvement.

Getty-Dubay® Pre-test/Post-test

INFORMAL ASSESSMENT OF STUDENT PROGRESS

The main purpose of handwriting instruction is to promote legibility so that we can communicate with others and ourselves.

PRE-TEST Before beginning BOOK C, ask the student to write the following sentence.

A quick brown fox jumps over the lazy dog.

1.

2.

3.

POST-TEST After completing BOOK C, ask the student to write the following sentence and today's date in basic or cursive italic.

A quick brown fox jumps over the lazy dog.

4.

5.

6.

Write today's date.

ASSESSMENT

- SHAPE: Each letter is similar to the models in the workbook.
- SIZE: Similar letters are the same height (for example: aec, dhk, gpy). Capital letters and lowercase letters with ascenders are the same height.
- SLOPE: Letters have a consistent letter slope (between 5° – 15°).
- SPACING: Letters within words are closely spaced. Spaces between words are the width of **n**.
- SPEED: Words are written fluently at a comfortable speed.

(Teacher: see INSTRUCTION MANUAL)

GETTY-DUBAY® BASIC ITALIC LOWERCASE FAMILIES
presented according to similar shapes

INSTRUCTOR: Have student complete Pre-test on Page viii.

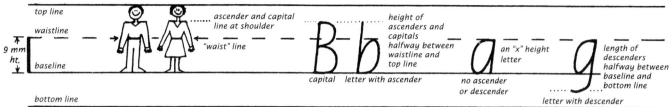

• Lowercase Families •

FAMILY 1: **i, j, l** family — straight line downstroke

INSTRUCTOR: Review one family at a time.

Trace letters:

1.

Trace letters, then write your own at the dots:

2.

Write your own Family 1 letters:

3.

FAMILY 2: **k, v, w, x, z** family — diagonal line

4.

Trace letters, then write your own at the dots:

5.

Write your own Family 2 letters:

6.

LOOK: ✏ Circle your best letter on line 6.   Did you circle a letter on line 6? ✏ yes   no

9mm

Getty-Dubay® Italic Handwriting Series • Book C   © 2020 Handwriting Success

Getty-Dubay® Basic Italic Lowercase Families

FAMILY 3: **h**, **m**, **n**, **r** family — arch   INSTRUCTOR: Review one family at a time.

Trace letters:

1 h h m m n n r r

Trace letters, then write your own at the dots:

2 h m n r

Write your own Family 3 letters:

3

Read the words on line 4, then trace them.

4 hill   mill   will

On line 5, write the words you traced on line 4.

5 h   m   w

FAMILY 4: **u**, **y** family — inverted arch

6 u u   y y

Trace letters, then write your own at the dots:

7 u   y

Read the word on line 8 and trace it. Then write the word at the dots:

8 run   run

LOOK: Are your arches of **h**, **n** and **m** touching the waistline?   Circle one: yes   no

Getty-Dubay® Basic Italic Lowercase Families

FAMILY 5: **a, d, g, q** family — basic a shape   INSTRUCTOR: Review one family at a time.

Trace letters:

1   a a   d d   g g   q q

Trace letters, then write your own at the dots:

2   a   d   g   q

Read the words on line 3, then trace them.

3   glad   did   hug

On line 4, write the words you traced on line 3.

4   g   d   h

FAMILY 6: **b, p** family — inverted basic a shape

5   b b   p p

Trace letters, then write your own at the dots:

6   b   p

Read the words on line 7, then trace them.

7   Look! A big rabbit.

On line 8, write the words you traced on line 7.

8   L

LOOK: Are your letters close together in the words you wrote on line 8?   Circle one: yes   no

Getty-Dubay® Basic Italic Lowercase Families

FAMILY 7: **o, e, c, s** family — elliptical curve INSTRUCTOR: Review one time at a time.

Trace letters:

1 [o o e e c c s s

alternate 2-stroke e

Trace letters, then write your own at the dots:

2 [o . . e . . c . . s .

FAMILY: 8: **f, t** family — crossbar

3 [f f t t

t has a short ascender

4 [f . . t

fox

dog

Read the words on line 5, then trace them:

This sentence has all 26 letters in it. It is called a pangram.

5 [A quick brown fox

On line 6, write the words you traced on line 5:

6 [A

Read, then trace:

7 [jumps over the lazy dog.

Write the words you traced on line 7:

8 [j

LOOK: Read the sentence you wrote. ✏ Circle your best word. Did you circle your best word? ✏ yes no

Getty-Dubay® Basic Italic Lowercase

Trace, then write: · **Ways People Travel** · *Write your best letter in the box.*

1. a   a a a   a

2. automobile

3. b   b b b   b

4. bicycle

5. c   c c c   c

6. camel

Bactrian camel

7. d   d d d   d

8. donkey

LOOK: Does your a shape in a and d look happy ☺ or sad? ☹ ?   Circle one: a a

Getty-Dubay® Basic Italic Lowercase – Ways People Travel

Trace, then write: *Write your best letter in the box.*

1. e   e e e · · · · · e
   alternate 2-stroke e

2. elephant
   Asian elephant

3. f   f f f · · · · · f

4. ferry

5. g   g g g · · · · · g

6. glider

7. h   h h h · · · · · h

8. helicopter

LOOK: Are you closing your **g** at the top? ✏ Circle one: yes no

Getty-Dubay® Basic Italic Lowercase – Ways People Travel

Trace, then write: *Write your best letter in the box.*

1. i
2. ice skates
3. j
4. jet
5. k
6. kayak
7. l
8. llama

LOOK: Do most of your l's slant to the right the same way?   Circle one: yes   no

Getty-Dubay® Basic Italic Lowercase – Ways People Travel

Trace, then write: *Write your best letter in the box.*

1. m   m m m   m

2. motorcycle

3. n   n n n   n

4. norimon

   You'll need a BIG dictionary to find this word!

5. o   o o o   o

6. oxcart

   oxcart

7. p   p p p   p

8. pedicab

LOOK: Are you closing your **o** at the top?   Circle one: yes   no

Getty-Dubay® Basic Italic Lowercase – Ways People Travel

Trace, then write: Write your best letter in the box.

1. q   q q q   q

A ship uses this in a harbor. This word sounds like "key" and rhymes with "me."

2. quay

3. r   r r r   r

4. raft

5. s   s s s   s

6. subway

subway

7. t   t t t   t

8. toboggan

LOOK: Are you crossing each **t** on the waistline?   Circle one: yes   no

Getty-Dubay® Basic Italic Lowercase – Ways People Travel

Trace, then write: Fill each line!   Write your best letter in the box.

1. u u u u — — — — — u

2. umiak — — — —

3. v v v v — — — — — v

4. victoria — — —

victoria

5. w w w w — — — — — w

6. wagon — — — —

7. x x x x — — — — — x

Have your teacher help you find what a xebec is.

8. xebec — — — —

LOOK: Is your **w** touching the waistline three times?   Circle one: yes no

Getty-Dubay® Basic Italic Lowercase – Ways People Travel

Trace, then write: *Write your best letter in the box.*

1. y   y y y   y

2. yacht

3. z   z z z   z

4. zeppelin

zeppelin

5. We can travel in

6. many different ways.

Copy lines 5 and 6:

7.

8.

LOOK: How many ways have you traveled? ✏ _____ .

GETTY-DUBAY® BASIC ITALIC CAPITALS & LOWERCASE
Names of People

Trace, then write: Write your best letter in the box.

1. A A A · · · · · A

2. Aataq

3. B B B · · · · · B

4. Betty

5. C C C · · · · C

6. Carol

flower design, 15th c.

7. D D D · · · · D

8. David

LOOK: Are your capitals starting halfway between the waistline and the top line?   Circle one: yes   no

Getty-Dubay® Basic Italic Capitals and Lowercase – Names of People

Trace, then write: *Write your best letter in the box.*

1. I   I I
2. Inga
   border design, 14th c.
3. J   J J
4. Juanita
5. K   K K
6. Kurt
7. L   L L
8. Lloyd

LOOK: Does your second stroke of **K** form a 90° angle? Circle one: yes no
(A 90° angle is the same as a corner of a piece of notebook paper.)

Getty-Dubay® Basic Italic Capitals and Lowercase – Names of People

Trace, then write: Write your best letter in the box.

1. M M M M M

2. My-Ling

3. N N N N N

4. Norman

Celtic spiral, 9th c.

5. O O O O

6. Olive

7. P P P P

8. Peter

LOOK: Are your capitals starting halfway between the waistline and the top line?   yes   no

Getty-Dubay® Basic Italic Capitals and Lowercase – Names of People

Trace, then write: *Write your best letter in the box.*

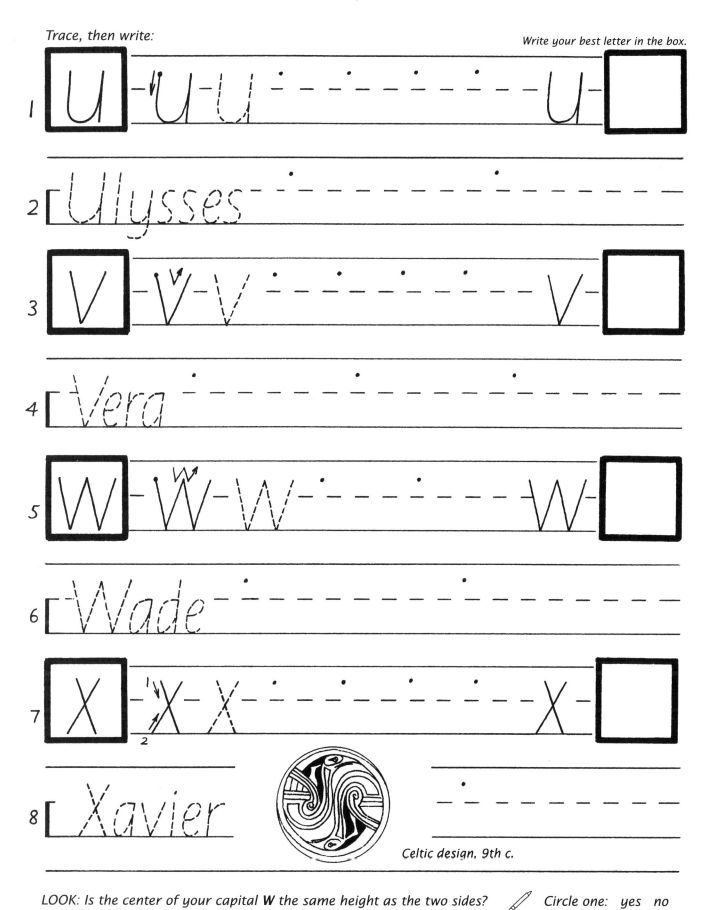

Celtic design, 9th c.

LOOK: Is the center of your capital **W** the same height as the two sides?   Circle one: yes   no

Getty-Dubay® Basic Italic Capitals and Lowercase – Names of People

Trace, then write: *Write your best letter in the box.*

1. Y   Y Y Y ········· Y

2. Yolanda

border design, 15th c.

3. Z   Z Z ········· Z

4. Zetta

Write your own capital above each of the small capitals:

5. A
   A   B   C   D   E   F

6.
   G   H   I   J   K   L   M

7.
   N   O   P   Q   R   S   T

8.
   U   V   W   X   Y   Z

LOOK: Are your capitals starting about halfway between the waistline and the top line?

Circle one: yes   no

Getty-Dubay® Basic Italic – Word Endings

Read, trace, then write: Word endings of **-s**, **-ing** and **-ed**

1. Nathan picks an apple.

Copy sentence from line 1:

2.

3. Are Jack and Jill
4. picking cherries?

Copy sentence from lines 3 and 4:

5.

6.

7. Sally picked a plum.

Copy sentence from line 7:

8.

LOOK: Do most of your letters slant the same way? a l k n y   Circle one: yes   no

GETTY-DUBAY® NUMERALS & NUMBER WORDS

Trace, then write:

0   0 0   zero

1   1 1   one

2   2 2   two

3   3 3   three

4   4 4   four

5   5 5   five
   or 5

6   6 6   six

7   7 7   seven

INSTRUCTOR: Numerals may also be written at the same height as capitals. (See page v.)

Trace, then write:

8 `8  8  · · · · eight ·`

9 `9  9  · · · · nine`

10 `10  10  · · · · ten ·`

Just trace this sentence. Fill the blank with a word.

11 `I am _____ years old.`

Trace this sentence, then write it on lines 14 and 15:

12 `On my next birthday`

13 `I will be _____ years old.`

write a number

Copy lines 12 and 13:

14

15

LOOK: Did you fill in the blanks on line 11 and line 13?   Circle one: yes   no

Getty-Dubay® Basic – Question & Answer Sentences

Read, trace, then write: question and answer sentences

1 How many days are

2 there in a week?

Copy lines 1 and 2:

3

4

5 There are _____ days
              fill in a number

6 in every week.

Copy lines 5 and 6:

7

8

LOOK: Are you closing your **a** and **g** at the waistline?   Circle one: yes no

Months of the Year

Trace, then write:

1. January
2. February
3. March
4. April
5. May
6. June

A POEM:

January brings the snow,
   Makes our feet and fingers glow.
February brings the rain,
   Thaws the frozen lake again.
March brings breezes loud and shrill,
   Stirs the dancing daffodil.

April brings the primrose sweet,
   Scatters daisies at our feet.
May brings flocks of pretty lambs,
   Skipping by their fleecy dams.
June brings tulips, lilies, roses,
   Fills the children's hands with posies.

Trace, then write:

7. July
8. August
9. September
10. October
11. November
12. December

Hot <u>July</u> brings cooling showers,
   Apricots and gillyflowers.
<u>August</u> brings the sheaves of corn,
   Then the harvest home is borne.
Warm <u>September</u> brings the fruit,
   Sportsmen then begin to shoot.

Fresh <u>October</u> brings the pheasant,
   Then to gather nuts is pleasant.
Dull <u>November</u> brings the blast,
   Then the leaves are whirling fast.
Chill <u>December</u> brings the sleet,
   Blazing fire and holiday treat.
                MOTHER GOOSE

Getty-Dubay® Basic italic Capitals & Lowercase – Sentence Practice

❋ Seasons of the Year ❋

declarative and interrogative sentences

Read, then trace:

1. Spring is warm.

Copy line 1:

2.

3. Is summer hot?   Circle one: yes   no

Copy line 3:

4.

5. Autumn is cool.

Copy line 5:

6.

7. Is winter cold?   Circle one: yes   no

Copy line 7:

8.

Getty-Dubay® Basic italic Capitals & Lowercase – Sentence Practice

*positive, comparative & superlative forms of the adjective **big***

Read, trace, then write:

1 A lion is a big animal.

Copy line 1.

2

LOOK! This sentence has two lines:

3 A hippopotamus is a

4 bigger animal.

Copy lines 3 and 4:

5

6

7 Is the elephant biggest?*

WRITE: Yes, it is the biggest. OR WRITE: No, it is not the biggest.

8

*The elephant is the biggest land animal. The whale is the biggest animal.

Trace, then write: Quotations

1. Begin your day with
2. a smile!

Make a smiling face

Copy lines 1 and 2:

3.

4.

5. A friend is a present
6. you give yourself.

Copy lines 5 and 6:

7.

8.

LOOK: Are you starting your **d** at the waistline?   Circle one: yes   no

Getty-Dubay® Basic Italic Capitals & Lowercase

GETTY-DUBAY® BASIC ITALIC REVIEW

These letters are smaller. Trace the letters before writing your own.

1 | a b c d e f g h i j k l m n
Copy line 1:

2 |
Trace:

3 | o p q r s t u v w x y z
Copy line 3:

4 |
Trace:

5 | A B C D E F G H I J K L
Copy line 5:

6 |
Trace:

7 | M N O P Q R S T U V
Copy line 7:

8 |
Trace

9 | W X Y Z . , ? !
Copy line 9:

10 |
Trace:

11 | The alphabet has ___ letters.
Copy line 11:   *how many?*

12 |

INSTRUCTOR: First page using 6mm lines.

GETTY-DUBAY® NUMERALS & NUMBER WORDS

Trace, then write:

0   0 0   zero zero

1   1 1   one one

2   2 2   two two

3   3 3   three three

4   4 4   four four

5   5 5   five five

6   6 6   six six

7   7 7   seven seven

8   8 8   eight eight

9   9 9   nine nine

10 10 10   ten ten

11 11 11   eleven eleven

LOOK: Are you closing your **0, 5, 8** and **9** at the top?   Circle one: yes no
Are you closing the counter of **6**?   Circle one: yes no

Getty-Dubay® Numerals & Number Words

Trace, then write:

12 | 12 12 | twelve twelve

13 | 13 13 | thirteen

14 | 14 14 | fourteen

15 | 15 15 | fifteen

16 | 16 16 | sixteen

17 | 17 17 | seventeen

18 | 18 18 | eighteen

19 | 19 19 | nineteen

20 | 20 20 | twenty

21 | 100 | one hundred

22 | 1,000 | one thousand

23 | 1,000,000 | one million

Trace, then write:

1. Betty Botter bought some bitter
2. butter.
3.
4.
5. Does this shop stock shortstop
6. socks?
7.
8.
9. Peter Piper picked a peck of
10. pickled peppers.
11.
12.

LOOK: Are you bumping the baseline and waistline with the small letters like **a, c, e, m, o** and **s**?
Circle one: yes   no

Getty-Dubay® Basic Italic Sentence Practice – Tongue Twisters

Trace, then write:

1. She sells seashells by the
2. seashore.
3. S
4.
5. Three gray geese graze in the
6. green grass.
7. T
8.
9. Does double bubble gum
10. bubble double?
11. D
12.

LOOK: How many sets of double letters can you find on this page?

A contraction is a short word made from two other words.

1. cannot – can't • do not – don't

Copy line 1:

2.

Write a contraction from line 1 in the blank space:

3. Ellen _____ find her pencil.

Copy line 3:

4.

5. will not – won't • has not – hasn't

Copy line 5:

6.

Write a contraction from line 5 in the blank space:

7. Juan _____ gone to lunch.

Copy line 7:

8.

9. is not – isn't • does not – doesn't

Copy line 9:

10.

Write a contraction from line 9 in the blank space:

11. Gail _____ like to climb trees.

Copy line 11:

12.

LOOK: Did you fill in the blanks on lines 3, 7 and 11?   Circle one: yes   no

Getty-Dubay® Basic Italic – Homophones

Homophones sound alike but have different meanings and are spelled differently.

1. know – no • right – write

Copy line 1:

2.

Fill in the blanks with homophones from line 1:

3. I _____ how to _____ my name.

4.

5. meat – meet • ate – eight

Copy line 5:

6.

Fill in the blanks with homophones from line 5:

7. I will _____ you at _____ o'clock.

8.

9. be – bee • flour – flower

Copy line 9:

10.

Fill in the blanks with homophones from line 9:

11. The _____ buzzes near the _____.

Copy line 11:

12.

Getty-Dubay® Basic Italic – Compound Words

Write the two words that are used to make each compound word:

A word that is made by putting two smaller words together is called a compound word.

1. sailboat
   Trace the compound word above, then write it below.
   s + b

2. doghouse
   ___ + ___

3. beehive
   ___ + ___

4. raincoat
   ___ + ___

5. cookbook
   ___ + ___

6. mailbox
   ___ + ___

Getty-Dubay® Basic Italic – Compound Words

Fill in the blanks using compound words from page 36.

1. Bees live in a _____.
2. B
3. I need a _____ when it rains.
4. I
5. Have you sailed on a _____?
6. H
7. The dog is in his _____.
8. T
9. I put my letter in the _____.
10. I
11. Mother uses a _____ to cook.
12. M

LOOK: Are you keeping your letters close together in each word?   Circle one: yes   no

TRANSITION TO GETTY-DUBAY® CURSIVE ITALIC

Trace, then write:

1. Serifs are lines added to letters.

2.

EXIT SERIFS:

3. a becomes a   d becomes d   h becomes h   i becomes i

4. k becomes k   t becomes t   m becomes m   n becomes n

5. u becomes u   x becomes x   z becomes z

6. a a   d d   h h   i i

7. k k   t t   m m   n n

8. u u   x x   z z

9. Exit serifs are soft angle serifs.

10.

Getty-Dubay® Cursive Italic Lowercase Joins

ENTRANCE SERIFS: Trace, then write:

Four entrance serifs are soft angles.

3 n becomes n (soft angle entrance serif, exit serif), m becomes m, r becomes r (slightly bend arm of r), x becomes x

4 nn mm rr xx

LOOK: Are your entrance serifs on n m r and x soft angles? ✏ Circle one: yes   no

5 Four entrance serifs are sharp angles.

6

7 j becomes j (sharp angle entrance serif), p becomes p, v becomes v, w becomes w

8 jj pp vv ww

LOOK: Are your entrance serifs on j p v and w sharp angles? ✏ Circle one: yes   no

9 NOTE: f adds a descender f becomes f f f

INSTRUCTOR: If a student has difficulty with the transition to cursive italic, allow that student to continue with basic italic. Some students may enjoy using the exit serifs shown on pages 38 and 39 without using the joins on the following pages.

Getty-Dubay® Cursive Italic Lowercase Serifs

EXIT SERIFS: These eight letters only have soft angle exit serifs. (**m**, **n** and **x** also have exit serifs - see page 41)
Trace, then write:.

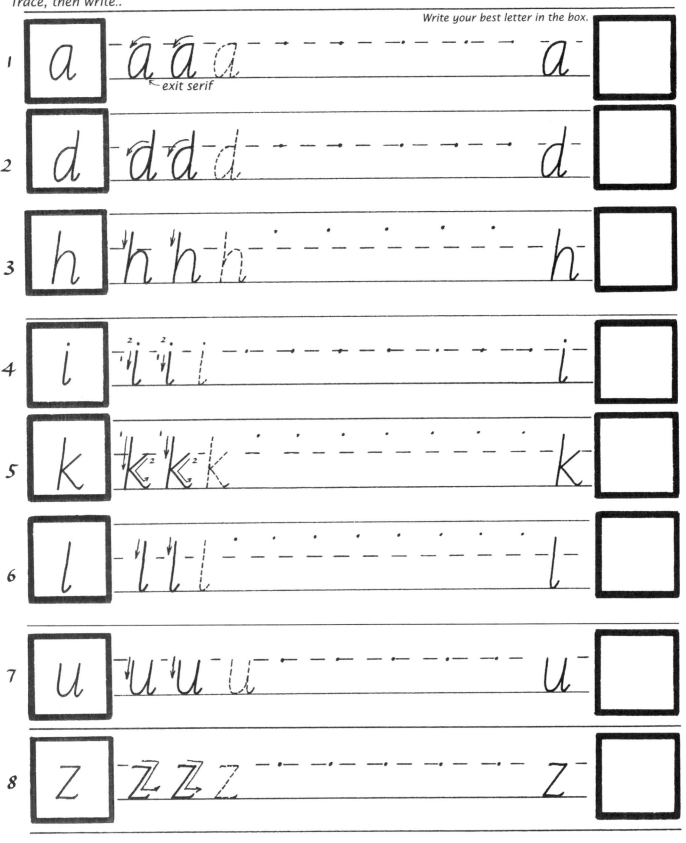

LOOK: Are you using a soft angle on your exit serifs?   Circle one: yes   no

Getty-Dubay® Cursive Italic Lowercase Serifs

ENTRANCE & EXIT SERIFS: **m**, **n** and **x** begin with a soft angle serif and end with a soft angle serif.

Write your best letter in the box.

1. m — entrance serif / exit serif — m m m · · · · · m

2. n — entrance serif / exit serif — n n n · · · · · n

3. x — x x x · · · · · x

ENTRANCE SERIF: NOTE: **r** begins with a soft angle serif.

4. r — r r r ← Bend arm of **r** down slightly for cursive italic. · · · · · · r

ENTRANCE SERIFS: These four letters begin with a sharp angle serif.

5. j — j j j · · · · · j

6. p — p p p · · · · · p

7. v — v v v · · · · · v

8. w — w w w · · · · · w

Getty-Dubay® Italic Handwriting Series · Book C © 2020 Handwriting Success

Getty-Dubay® Cursive Italic Lowercase – Join 1

JOIN 1: Diagonal Join into n Join with diagonal, then roll over into soft angle entrance serif of **n**.

1. an an an an
   Serifs are like hands reaching out to join another letter.
   fill the box with your **an**

Trace, then write:

2. an   en   in
3. kn   mn   un
4. funny   sand
5. Jan made a funny sandman.   ← this is shown in line 8

Copy line 5:
6.

JOIN 1: Diagonal Join into m. Join with diagonal, then roll over into soft angle entrance serif of **m**.

7. am am am am
   Trace, then write:

8. am   em
9. im   um
10. plum   thumb
11. Sam had a plum on his thumb.

Copy line 11:
12.

JOIN 1: diagonal to form soft angle into **n, m, r, x** out of **a, c, d, e, h, i, k, l, m, n, u, z**
LOOK: Are you joining the letters that have lines under them?   Circle one: yes   no

Getty-Dubay® Italic Handwriting Series · Book C   © 2020 Handwriting Success

Getty-Dubay® Cursive Italic Lowercase – Join 1

JOIN 1: Diagonal Join into **r**.   Join with diagonal, then roll over into soft angle entrance serif of **r**.

1. ar   ar ar   ar
   Trace the large writing to get the feel of the join before writing smaller.

2. ar   er   ir

3. kr   mr   ur

4. campfire   burn

5. The campfire is burning.
   Copy line 5:

6.

JOIN 1: Diagonal Join into **x**.   Join with diagonal, then roll over into soft angle entrance serif of **x**.

7. ax   ax ax   ax
   Trace, then write:

8. ax   ex   ix

9. kx   mx   ux

10. Max   six axes   one ax!

11. Max sharpened Tina's six axes.
    Copy line 11:

12.

LOOK: Are you joining the letters that have lines under them?   Circle one: yes   no

Getty-Dubay® Cursive Italic Lowercase – Join 2

JOIN 2: Diagonal Swing Up – Optional Join into n.

1. an | an an | an

Join into **n** halfway between baseline and waistline.

Trace, then write:

2. an — en — in

3. kn — nn — un

4. funny — sand

← this is shown in line 8

5. Jan made a funny sandman.

Copy line 5:

6.

JOIN 2: Diagonal Swing Up – Optional Join into m.

7. am | am am | am

Join into **m** halfway between baseline and waistline.

8. am — em — im

9. mm — um

10. plum — 🌱 thumb

11. Sam had a plum on his thumb.

Copy line 11:

12.

JOIN 2: diagonal swing up to form sharp angle into **b, h, i, j, k, l, p, t, u, v, w, y**; option into **m, n, r, x** from any letter with an exit serif and **c, e**

Getty-Dubay® Cursive Italic Lowercase – Join 2

JOIN 2: Diagonal Swing Up – Optional Join into r.

1. ar ar ar ar
   Join into r halfway between baseline and waistline.

Trace, then write:

2. ar   er   ir

3. kr   nr   ur

4. campfire   burn

5. The campfire is burning.

Copy line 5:

6.

JOIN 2: Diagonal Swing Up – Optional Join into x. Join into x to form sharp angle.

7. ax ax ax ax

8. ax   ex   ix

9. kx   nx   ux

10. Max   six axes

11. Max sharpened Tina's six axes.

Copy line 11:

12.

LOOK: Are you joining the letters that have lines under them?   Circle one: yes   no

Getty-Dubay® Cursive Italic Lowercase - Join 2

JOIN 2: Diagonal Swing Up into i.   Join into i halfway between baseline and waistline.

1. ai ai ai ai

Trace, then write:
2. ai   di   ki
3. li   mi   ni   zi

(this join on next page)
4. kite   high

5. Toni's kite flew high in the sky.

Copy line 5:
6.

JOIN 2: Diagonal Swing Up into p.   Join into p halfway between baseline and waistline.

7. ap ap ap ap

Trace, then write:
8. ap   lp   up
9. happy   slip   help
10. jump   up   lap

Read, then trace:
11. Flip jumped up on Cap's lap.

Copy line 11:
12.

JOIN 2: diagonal swing up to form sharp angle into **b, h, i, j, k, l, p, t, u, v, w, y**; option into **m, n, r, x** from any letter with an exit serif and **c, e**

Getty-Dubay® Cursive Italic Lowercase – Join 2

JOIN 2: Diagonal Swing Up into t. Join into **t** halfway between baseline and waistline.

1. at | at at | at

Trace, then write:

2. at | dt | it
3. kt | nt | ut
4. plate | fact | kite

Read then trace:

5. Pat built her own paper kite.

Copy line 5:

6.

JOIN 2: Diagonal Swing Up into u. Join into **u** halfway between baseline and waistline.

7. au | au au | au

Trace then write:

8. au | du
9. lu | nu
10. Paul | lunch

Read, then trace:

11. Paul ate too much lunch today. *(this join on next page)*

Copy line 11:

12.

JOIN 2: Diagonal Swing Up into **v** and **w**. Join into **v** and **w** to form sharp angle.

1. av   av av   av

Trace, then write:
2. av   w   have
3. live   save   five
4. aw   aw aw   aw
5. aw   dw   saw
6. draw   hawk

Can you draw a hawk?

JOIN 2: Diagonal Swing Up into **y** & **j**. Join into **y** & **j** halfway between baseline and waistline.

7. ay   ay ay   ay
8. ay   ly   ny
9. play   sunny
10. aj aj aj   aj
11. aj   aj   ajar

Copy sentence here:
12. The door is ajar.

Getty-Dubay® Cursive Italic Lowercase – Join 2

JOIN 2: Diagonal Swing Up into b. Join into **b** halfway between baseline and waistline.

1. ab ab ab ab

Trace, then write:

2. ab   ib   ub

3. cab   bib   cub

JOIN 2: Diagonal Swing Up into h. Join into **h** halfway between baseline and waistline.

4. ah ah ah ah

Trace, then write:

5. ah   ih   uh

JOIN 2: Diagonal Swing Up into k. Join into **k** halfway between baseline and waistline.

6. ck ck ck ck

Trace, then write:

7. Pack a backpack.

JOIN 2: Diagonal Swing Up into l. Join into **l** halfway between baseline and waistline.

8. al al al al

Trace, then write:

9. al   el   il

10. A school bus is yellow.

11.

LOOK: When you join into an ascender, are you making a single line with no loop?   Circle one: yes no

Getty-Dubay® Cursive Italic Lowercase – Joins 3 & 4

JOIN 3: Diagonal into o. Join with a straight diagonal line, then start back into o.

1 stroke:
1. no   no no   no

Trace, then write:
2. co co   do do   to

3. mo   no   • coat

4. dog   how   took

JOIN 4: Diagonal into e. Join with a straight diagonal line into e.

5. ne   ne ne   ne

Trace, then write:
6. ce   de   ee

7. he   ie   ke

DO trace the sentence before you write it yourself on line 9.

8. Shelley has one pet hen.

one hen

9.

Trace, then write the sentence on line 11:

nest
10. The bluebird built a nest.

11.

JOIN: 3: diagonal into **o** from the baseline from any letter with an exit serif and **c, e**
JOIN 4: diagonal into **e** from the baseline from any letter with an exit serif and **c, e**

LOOK: Are you making a straight line when joining into **o** and **e**?   Circle one: yes   no

Getty-Dubay® Cursive Italic Lowercase – Join 5

JOIN 5: Horizontal out of f.   Join with a straight horizontal line out of the crossbar of f.

1. fa   fa fa   fa

Trace, then write:

2. fa   fi   fo   fs

3. fan   fat   for   *this join on next page*

4. fig   find

5. Did Fran find a fat fig?

three figs

Copy line 5:

6.

JOIN 5: Horizontal out of t.   Join with a straight horizontal line out of the crossbar of t.

7. ta   ta ta   ta

8. ta   ti   tu

9. twins   tan   hats

10. The twins have tan hats.

Copy line 10:

11.

JOIN 5: Horizontal out of x.   Join with a straight horizontal line out of x.

12. xi   xi xi   exit

JOIN 5: horizontal out of **f, t, x, o, v, w** into all letters except **f** — optional into **e**

Getty-Dubay® Cursive Italic Lowercase – Join 5

JOIN 5: Horizontal out of o. Join with a straight horizontal line out of **o**.

1. oa oa oa oa

   Reach out along the waistline.

2. oa   od   ou

3. The boat is out in the ocean.

Copy line 3:

4.

JOIN 5: Horizontal out of v & w. Join with a straight horizontal line out of **v & w**.

5. va va va va

6. va   ve *or ve*   vi

7. van   vet *or ve*

8. pave *or ve*   have *or ve*

9. wa wa wa wa

10. wa   we *or we*   wi

11. We *or we* went along the waterway.

Copy line 11:

12.

INSTRUCTOR: When joining "horizontally" into **e**, curve downward instead of writing a horizontal line.
In BOOK C, lift after **f** and **t** when followed by **e**.

REVIEW: GETTY-DUBAY® CURSIVE ITALIC LOWERCASE JOINS 1-5

Trace, then write:

JOIN 1:
1. an an am   ar   ax

JOIN 2:
OPTION: Join into **n, m, r** and **x**.
2. an an am   ar   ax

3. au au ay   ai   aj

4. ap ap av   aw   at

5. at at ah   ak   ab

JOIN 3:   **JOIN 4:**
6. ao ao ae ae

JOIN 5:
7. oa oa ta

fox   dog

8. fa fa va   wa   xa

9. A pangram: A quick brown fox
   (or an)   *(or am)*

10.

11. jumps over the lazy dog.
    (or um)   *(or ver)*

12.

LIFTS: Lift before **f** and **z**; lift after **g, j, q** and **y**.

Have your teacher write your name in cursive italic on line 1:

1.

Write your name in cursive italic on line 2:

2.

Trace, then write:

3. I am learning cursive italic.

Copy line 3:

4.

This is an alphabet sentence, also called a pangram. Can you find all 26 letters in it?

5. The wild lizard jumped quickly

Copy line 5:

6.

7. over seven frog boxes.

Copy line 7:

8.

9. Quincy and Meg waved goodbye

Copy line 9:

10.

11. and blasted off for Planet Zero.

Copy line 11:

12.

LOOK: Four of the 26 letters of our alphabet are missing in this sentence on lines 9 and 11. Can you list them? ____ ____ ____ ____

GETTY-DUBAY® BASIC ITALIC CAPITALS & CURSIVE ITALIC JOINS 1-5
Cities of the United States

Trace, then write:

1. A A Atlanta — GA*
2. B Billings — MT
3. C Concord — NH
4. D Denver — CO
5. E Evanston — IL
6. F Flagstaff — AZ
7. G Gettysburg — PA
8. H Honolulu — HI
9. I Idaho Falls — ID
10. J Juneau — AK
11. K Kansas City — KS·MO
12. L Lansing — MI

*State abbreviation. Other states may have cities or towns with the same names as listed on pages 55, 56 and 57.

Getty-Dubay® Basic Italic Capitals & Cursive Italic Lowercase – Cities of the United States

LOOK: Have you been to any of these cities? Circle one: yes   no

Trace, then write:

1. M M   Madison — WI
2. N   Nashville — TN
3. O   Ogden — UT
4. P   Portland — OR
5. Q   Quincy — MA
6. R   Richmond — VA
7. S   Sunnyvale — CA
8. T   Trenton — NJ
9. U   Utica — NY
10. V   Vancouver — WA
11. W   Wilmington — DE
12. X   X

LOOK: Can you find a city that begins with the letter X? Circle one: yes   no
(Ask your teacher to help you.)

Getty-Dubay® Basic Italic Capitals & Cursive Italic Lowercase – Cities of the United States

LOOK: Do you live in a city?   Circle one: yes   no

1. Y Y Yankton
   SD

2. Z Zapata
   TX

3. A city is a large town.
Copy line 3:

4.

5. Some cities are larger than
6. others.
Copy lines 5 and 6:

7.

8.
You may need help to find the answer for this next sentence:

9. The largest city in the United
10. States is   .
Copy lines 9 and 10:

11.

12.

LOOK: Are you joining all of the letters that are underlined?   Circle one: yes   no

Getty-Dubay® Basic Italic Capitals & Cursive Italic Lowercase – Sentence Practice

JOINS PRESENTED IN BOOK C: JOINS 1, 2, 3, 4 and 5   *Joins 6, 7 and 8 are introduced in BOOK D.

n anbn cn dn en fn gn hn in jn kn l n mn
nn on pn qn r n s n t n un vn wn xn yn zn

The writer may join any letter to another.   EXCEPTION: Lift before **f** and **z**, lift after **g, j, q** and **y**.

1 Happiness is having a friend.

2

3 Happiness is going to the zoo.

4

Write your own ending:

5 Happiness is

6

7 Happiness is completing Book C!

8

Hooray for you!
Now that you have completed Book C, turn to page viii to write the Post-test.
This will be an example of your "personal best" handwriting.
If you see an improvement in your handwriting, give yourself a star!

Congratulations!

A Favorite Letter

1. In the space above, write a favorite cursive lowercase letter. (Make a large one with a crayon, colored pencil or pen.)

2. Anywhere in the space above, write words that have your letter in them. Use the joins you know. *(Write with a pencil or pen.)*

3. In the space above or on your own paper, use some of your words to write a sentence.

4. On your own paper, draw a picture about your sentence.*

*Instructor note: This activity might be completed during the next handwriting session.

SUPPLEMENT TO GETTY-DUBAY® ITALIC HANDWRITING SERIES BOOK C
READING LOOPED CURSIVE
Prerequisite: *Student familiarity with cursive italic*

Sometimes you will see handwriting in styles other than your own italic handwriting.
You can use the skills you have learned already to read the **looped cursive** style of handwriting.

Looped Cursive

LOOPED CURSIVE LOWERCASE

These looped cursive lowercase letters are similar to cursive italic.

*Note: Your italic t should not extend as high as this looped cursive one.

	Read each looped cursive letter.	Read the word.	Read the word written quickly.	Write the word in cursive italic.
1	a	ant*	ant	a ant
2	c o	cocoon	cocoon	co
3	d i	dime	dime	di
4	u	until	until	u
5	m n	many	many	mn
6	e	even	even	e

These letters have long looped descenders.

	Read each looped cursive letter.	Read the word.	Read the word written quickly.	Write the word in cursive italic.
7	j g	juggle	juggle	jg juggle
8	p y	puppy	puppy	py
9	q	quiet	quiet	q

These letters have tall looped ascenders.

(See how they run into the line above?)

10	h	high	high	h
11	k	kick	kick	k
12	l	lilies	lilies	l

t is taller

| 13 | t t | tent | tent | t |

v & w are rounded

| 14 | v w | wave | wave | w |

x joins from the baseline.

These five looped cursive letters are different in shape from cursive italic. Learn to recognize them by sight (b, f, r, s, z).

	Read each looped cursive letter.	Read the word.	Read the word written quickly.	Write the word in cursive italic.
1	x	exit	exit	x exit
2	b	brief	brief	b
3	f	fluffy	fluffy	f
4	r	record	record	r
5	s	shows	shows	s
6	z	zigzag	zigzag	z

LOOPED CURSIVE CAPITALS

Many looped cursive capitals look like italic capitals (*B, C, D, E, H, K, O, P, R, U, V, W, X*). Review all italic capitals by tracing the models on lines 7, 8 and 9 below.

B C D E H K O P R U V W X

7

These three looped cursive capitals look like lowercase letters (*A, M, N*).

A M N

8

Some looped cursive capitals are harder to read, but can be memorized (*F, G, I, J, L, Q, S, T, Z*).

F I J S L T Q Z

9

Read the name and write it below in cursive italic.

Fran   Janet   Sally

10

Gail   Larry   Tom

11

Ian   Quinn   Zack

12

Credit: The looped cursive font utlized above is Learning Curve by Blue Vinyl Fonts.

Getty-Dubay® – Letter Lines

1 date

2 salutation

3 body

4

5

6

7 closing

8 name

Place unlined sheet of paper over these lines when writing a rough draft or final copy of a letter.

This page may be reproduced for use with the
Getty-Dubay® Italic Handwriting Series.

© 2020 Handwriting Success
Getty-Dubay® Italic Handwriting Series
www.handwritingsuccess.com

Ruled Line Masters - 9mm

Name _____

1
2
3
4
5
6
7
8

Ruled Line Master - 7mm